SATISFY

my

THIRSTY SOUL

journal

LINDA DILLOW

A NavPress resource published in alliance
with Tyndale House Publishers

NavPress is the publishing ministry of The Navigators, an international Christian organization and leader in personal spiritual development. NavPress is committed to helping people grow spiritually and enjoy lives of meaning and hope through personal and group resources that are biblically rooted, culturally relevant, and highly practical.

For more information, visit NavPress.com.

Satisfy My Thirsty Soul Journal

Copyright © 2021 by Paniym Group, Inc. All rights reserved.
Copyright © 2007, 2021 by Linda Dillow. All rights reserved.

A NavPress resource published in alliance with Tyndale House Publishers

The Team for the second edition:
Don Pape, Publisher; Caitlyn Carlson, Editor; Elizabeth Schroll, Copy Editor; Julie Chen, Designer

Cover photograph of abstract art copyright © Mari Dein/Adobe Stock. All rights reserved.

Cover photograph of gold texture copyright © by Studio Denmark/Creative Market. All rights reserved.

Cover photograph of blue abstract painting copyright © Liliia/Adobe Stock. All rights reserved.

For information about special discounts for bulk purchases, please contact Tyndale House Publishers at csresponse@tyndale.com, or call 1-800-323-9400.

ISBN 978-1-64158-226-1

Printed in China

27   26   25   24   23   22   21
7   6   5   4   3   2   1

MORE LINDA DILLOW

Bestsellers

FROM NAVPRESS

Satisfy My Thirsty Soul

Calm My Anxious Heart

Calm My Anxious Heart Journal

A Deeper Kind of Calm

Intimacy Ignited

INTRODUCTION

Happy are those who hear the joyful call to worship,
for they will walk in the light of your presence,
LORD.
They rejoice all day long in your wonderful reputation.
They exult in your righteousness.
You are their glorious strength.
It pleases you to make us strong.

PSALM 89:15-17, NLT

Wonderful promises spill forth from Psalm 89. The verses declare that those who worship will walk in the light of God's presence. They will be filled with rejoicing over who God is all day long. They will delight in God's attributes, and the Lord God will become their strength—not just ordinary strength but *glorious* strength—because the Holy One delights to make His worshipers strong!

My friend, you hold in your hands the companion journal to *Satisfy My Thirsty Soul.* This is the third piece of the puzzle to encourage you to grow as a worshiper.

1. The book, *Satisfy My Thirsty Soul*, is an honest account of what I learned during my worship journey, combined with teaching and application to help you grow in living a lifestyle of worship.

2. The Bible study, located in the back of *Satisfy My Thirsty Soul*, takes you into Scripture so you can learn firsthand about worship. A major part of each Bible

study lesson is a "worship experience" designed to enhance and deepen your understanding of worship.

3. This *Satisfy My Thirsty Soul Journal* is a place for you to record what you discover during the worship experiences.

Maybe you're saying, "If I am reading a book and doing a Bible study, why do I need to journal?" It is a good question. Let me try to answer it.

The *Satisfy My Thirsty Soul Journal* not only acts as a historical record of your walk in the light of God's presence, it serves as a window into your soul. Your written words become an album of your thoughts, feelings, and experiences. As you chronicle, draw out, and reflect on who you are *becoming* as a worshiper, your worship experience will become more concrete.

Time to get started. The blank pages await you, not as a place to write pious prayers to God or to jot down what you think your Bible study leader wants to hear but as a place for you to spill out your soul. Go ahead and stain the pages with your tears. Or doodle delightful pictures on the margins. This is your space, your place, where you can be real. That means:

- ☺ you can misspell;
- ☺ you can be sloppy;
- ☺ you can write what you really feel;
- ☺ you can be real; and
- ☺ you can write sideways or upside down.

Here are other creative ideas that I really like from those I call "Super Journalers":

1. *Pray on paper.*
   Start with "Dear God" or "My Father" like you're

writing a love letter to Him. Write straight from your heart the concerns uppermost on your mind. Instead of concluding with "Amen," sign it, "Your Loving Daughter, (*your name*)."

2. *Think on paper.*
   Commit to embrace truth and reject lies about who God is and who you are.

3. *Sing on paper.*
   Allow your words to flow lyrically in unceasing fashion as David's words do in the Psalms.

4. *Feel on paper.*
   Be real! Don't be afraid to say, "This journaling stuff is hard," or "I never realized I was such a good writer."

5. *Draw on paper.*
   You don't have to be an artist! No matter your skill level, get some colored pencils or magic markers and give artistic creative expression a try. The sky's the limit. Scrapbook, sculpt, paint—use any medium.

6. *Document on paper.*
   Keep a record of what you have learned and how you have grown. Be sure to date each entry.

7. *Don't let perfection keep you from writing.*
   You aren't performing for anybody. Come just as you are.

8. *Try a new place.*
   Discover a new location. Journal as you sit in the sun—or, if you're brave, in the snow!

9. *Record your emotions.*
   What is your dominant emotion this week? Anxiety? Joy? Hope? Write about it.

SATISFY MY THIRSTY SOUL JOURNAL

10. *Thank God for revealing new things to you.*
    Do you ever say, "It hit me" or "I suddenly realized as I wrote . . ."? These insights are gifts from God, so thank Him for giving them to you.

11. *Ask probing questions.*
    Ask the hard questions. You don't have to have answers.

12. *Thank God you are growing.*
    Detail new ways you are growing as a worshiper.

The journal I kept during my adventure of growing as a worshiper is one of my most prized possessions because it holds a part of me. I often pull my journal off my shelf and read through the pages. As I do, my heart leaps with joy. I can see how I've grown. I remember wonderful encounters with my Father. My reading turns to worship and prayer as I reflect on the joy of discovering God's voice and delighting in His presence.

In *Experiencing God*, Henry Blackaby said, "If the God of the universe tells you something, you should write it down."[1] I am so thankful I wrote down my journey. This is why I feel passionately about you doing the same. I believe your journal will become a safe place where you can observe, reflect, understand, and move toward change.

I am convinced that if you faithfully read *Satisfy My Thirsty Soul*, study God's Word, and journal about your worship journey, at the end of the ten weeks you will say, "I have grown as a worshiper, and I am beginning to walk in the light of God's presence!"

Moses asked God to give the light of His presence for his journey to the Promised Land. God promised Moses that He would go with him. As you begin your journey, know that I am asking God to go with you and to be your ever-present Companion.

God's blessings on your journey!

Week One

MY
THIRSTY SOUL

MY THIRSTY SOUL

O God, you are my God,
earnestly I seek you;
my soul thirsts for you,
my body longs for you,
in a dry and weary land
where there is no water.

PSALM 63:1, NIV

I am excited that you have made the choice to go on your own worship journey! So much has changed in my life since I first began this journey:

- ⤸ God's presence has become my portion.
- ⤸ I am becoming a prayer warrior.
- ⤸ My joy is unspeakable.
- ⤸ I delight in intimacy with the Lord.

I was surprised to discover that God's presence is hidden in worship and that as I grow in worship, I also grow in intimacy with the Lord. Worship begins in holy expectancy that we will see God, and it ends in holy obedience. It is the response of a lover to her Beloved; it is the lifestyle of a grateful heart.

We all long for *into-me-see* oneness with someone. Here is what my friend Kathy told me:

> I thought I would find deep intimacy in my marriage, but since my husband and I were both emotionally crippled for the first decade or so of our marriage, our relationship did not meet *my* expectations. I'd always searched for a soul mate, but felt that my husband wouldn't ever be that person. I craved someone . . . anyone . . . to be able to find me and know me to the core of my being. I longed for it and searched for it in Christian friendships. However, nothing and no one ever seemed to truly satisfy the deep need to "be known" so intimately.[1]

The amazing news is that God intimately knows you and me, and He longs for us to know Him. The psalmist David said that the mighty God of the universe had searched and known him. God was intimately acquainted with all of David's ways (Psalm 139:1, 3). And the wonderful news is: Your ways are completely known to Him as well.

A TEN-MINUTE
WORSHIP EXPERIENCE

It is time for your first worship experience. Four or five days this week, worship God by declaring WHO HE IS.

Here are some suggestions for your worship time:

1. Put on worship music, bow or fall to your knees, and be still in God's presence for ten minutes. Ask God to teach you about intimacy with Him.
2. As you kneel before Him, read Psalm 63:1-8 out loud to God. Ask Him to teach you about who He is and how you can grow in your worship of Him.
3. Declare all the truths you find about God in these verses. Here are four; continue reading and you'll find more.

- ⌒ You are MY God.
- ⌒ You are powerful.
- ⌒ Your lovingkindness is better than life.
- ⌒ I am satisfied with you—more satisfied than with chocolate (Linda's paraphrase).

Look at David's worship responses. Here are four to get you started.

- ⌒ He thirsted and yearned for God.
- ⌒ He saw God.
- ⌒ His lips praised God.
- ⌒ He lifted his hands to God.

Write down what you thought or
felt during your time of worship.

MY DAILY REFLECTIONS

One thing I have asked from the LORD, that I shall seek:
That I may dwell in the house of the LORD all the days of
my life,
To behold the beauty of the LORD,
And to meditate in His temple.

PSALM 27:4

How lovely are Your dwelling places,
O LORD of Hosts!
My soul longed and even yearned for the courts of
the LORD;
my heart and my flesh sing for joy to the living God.

PSALM 84:1-2

Martha, Martha, you are worried and bothered about so many things; but only one thing is necessary, for Mary has chosen the good part, which shall not be taken away from her.

LUKE 10:41-42

_____

_____

_____

_____

_____

_____

_____

_____

_____

_____

_____

_____

_____

_____

_____

_____

_____

_____

Prayer is the occupation of the soul with its needs.
Praise is the occupation of the soul with its blessings.
Worship is the occupation of the soul with God
Himself. . . . "Lord, save my soul," is prayer.
"Thank you, Lord, for saving my soul," is praise.
"Thank you, Lord, for who you are," is worship.

—A. P. GIBBS

It is important to be able to say, This is who I am.
I am not primarily a worker for God. I am first
and foremost a lover of God. All of us need to
be lovers who work rather than workers who love.

—BOB SORGE

_____

_____

_____

_____

_____

_____

_____

_____

_____

_____

_____

_____

_____

_____

_____

_____

_____

_____

_____

_____

Lord, you are my Rock and my Redeemer. When my mouth is dry, I will drink of your Word. My body aches to feel your hug. Lord, I crave your love in a world that seems bone dry of your presence. I have known your intimacy in the secret place; I have beheld the power and glory of the King enthroned above. I long for your embrace, and my mouth will ever speak of your love. In holy worship, I lift my hands to the King; I will praise Him forever. My soul is like a vacuum filled only by your presence. My quivering voice sings praises to you, and you are my last thought as I drift off to sleep. I dream of you, Lord, and then you are my first thought in the morning. Because I find safety in you, I wish only to stay in your embrace.[2]

—JUDY BOOTH'S PARAPHRASE OF PSALM 63:1-8

My worship journey has turned me from a Martha into a Mary. Does this mean I no longer serve others? No! I serve *more*, but my service now flows from a different place:

> *My service flows from a heart saturated with worship.*
>
> *My service flows from a heart saturated with the presence of God.*

_____

_____

_____

_____

_____

_____

_____

_____

_____

_____

_____

_____

_____

_____

_____

_____

*Worship is the upspring of a heart that has known
the Father as a Giver, the Son as Savior,
and the Holy Spirit as the indwelling Guest.*

—A. P. GIBBS

WHAT DID I LEARN ABOUT
GOD THIS WEEK?

_____

_____

_____

_____

_____

_____

_____

_____

WHAT DID I LEARN ABOUT
MYSELF THIS WEEK?

_____

_____

_____

_____

_____

_____

_____

_____

WHAT DID I LEARN ABOUT
WORSHIP THIS WEEK?

_____

_____

_____

_____

_____

_____

_____

_____

MY PRAYER EXPRESSING HOPE
FOR MY WORSHIP JOURNEY:

_____

_____

_____

_____

_____

_____

_____

_____

_____

Week Two

MY WORSHIP
AWAKENING

Week Two

MY WORSHIP AWAKENING

---

*H*oly, Holy, Holy is the LORD of hosts,
The whole earth is full of His glory.
ISAIAH 6:3

One woman said this about the beginning of her journey to become a worshiper:

> I saw a woman in worship. Her face was lifted to heaven, graced with a beautiful expression of joy. I thought, *What does she know that I don't know?* This began my search to know more of God and to become a woman of worship.

Like this woman, I longed to wake up to worship. I was awake to God's Word but not to His voice and His presence. God opened my eyes, and I began to grow in awe, astonished wonder, and adoration. I discovered that worship is to: *adore, admire, celebrate, esteem, exult, glorify, love, magnify, praise, revere*, and *venerate* my holy God.

As I spent time on my knees in God's presence, I realized that when I adore Him, worship becomes a beautiful and personal love exchange between my God and me.

God awakened me to worship! I pray He awakens you, too.

THE ABCs OF WORSHIP

Worship God with the ABCs of Worship several times this week. I love to let my mind free-flow and think of all my God is. As I move from A–Z, I become overwhelmed. Our God is an awesome God!

Here are some ideas for this time:

1. Quiet your heart by listening to one or two worship songs.
2. Kneel, stand, or take a walk, and declare to God all He is. Beginning with the letter *A*, declare everything true of God that begins with *A*. Then move on to the letter *B*. If you need encouragement with the ABCs, look at Valerie's ABCs on page 27.
3. Write here about this worship time with God. What did you think, see, and feel? Was it hard, easy, or in between?

_____

_____

_____

_____

_____

_____

_____

_____

_____

_____

_____

_____

MY DAILY REFLECTIONS

*In worship I acknowledge my limitations.
In worship I also acknowledge that God
has no limitations. I bow before Him.
He is beyond me in everything.*

—WATCHMAN NEE

*I will give thanks to the L*ORD *with all my heart;*
I will tell of all Your wonders.
I will be glad and exult in You;
I will sing praise to Your name, O Most High.

PSALM 9:1-2

*Worship is meant to be a love exchange between
the bride of Christ and her beloved, Jesus.
It's not optional; it's essential.
In His glorious presence, every other
competing voice is hushed to a whisper.*

—BECKY HARLING

*To fall prostrate is beautifully reverent,
blowing kisses is delightfully relational.*

—SANDI

_____

_____

_____

_____

_____

_____

_____

_____

_____

_____

_____

_____

_____

_____

_____

_____

_____

_____

_____

_____

_____

_____

We are under obligation to make our devotion to God so attractive that all who see us lost in the wonder of our praise might desire to know the object of our praise.

—CALVIN MILLER

VALERIE'S ABCs OF WORSHIP

A: Alpha, Architect of Life, abounding in love, Angel Sender

B: Bountiful One, Banquet Host, Burden Lifter, Bondage Breaker

C: Chief Shepherd, Comforter, Compassionate One, Creator

D: Darkness Crusher, Death Defier, Defender, Deliverer

E: Encourager, Endurance Coach, enthralled by my beauty

F: Forever Friend, Father, Fear Remover, Final Destination

G: Grace Provider, Gentle Whisperer, Glorious One

H: healer of my body, Hand-Holder, Heart Restorer, Holy One

I: Invincible, Infirmity Eliminator, Immortal, Iniquity Eraser

J: Joy Giver, jealous for my affection

K: Keeper of my heart, Kind King, knows me

L: Light of the World, Lion of Judah, Life Giver, my complete lover

M: Miracle Worker, Most High, Majesty, Music Composer

N: never fails me, never forsakes me, Nature Designer

O: Omega, Opportunity Giver, Overcoming One

P: Patience Provider, Peace Maker, Passover Lamb, Perfect Physician

Q: Quencher of my thirst, quiets me with His love

R: resplendent with light, rejoices over me with singing

S: Super-Sized Super Hero, Salvation, Safe Haven, Shepherd, Shield

T: Trustworthy, Tear Wiper, testifies in my favor

U: unashamed of me, Unblemished One, understands me

V: Victorious One, voice I long for, Valley Elevator

W: Wonderful Counselor, Wound Healer, writes my name in heaven

X: expert in all the ways of me

Y: Yahweh, Youth Restorer

Z: zealous for His Holy Name, Zion Dweller

WHAT DID I LEARN ABOUT
GOD THIS WEEK?

_____

_____

_____

_____

_____

_____

_____

_____

WHAT DID I LEARN ABOUT
MYSELF THIS WEEK?

_____

_____

_____

_____

_____

_____

_____

_____

WHAT DID I LEARN ABOUT
WORSHIP THIS WEEK?

_____

_____

_____

_____

_____

_____

_____

_____

MY PRAYER EXPRESSING MY DESIRE
TO WAKE UP TO WORSHIP:

_____

_____

_____

_____

_____

_____

_____

_____

Week Three

MY SOUL FINDS
STILLNESS

MY SOUL FINDS

STILLNESS

Be still, and know that I am God.

PSALM 46:10, NIV

Stillness brings a deeper understanding of God and His ways. My prayer for you this week is that you will become comfortable with stillness. Intimacy with God was the hidden treasure I discovered in stillness.

Begin your time with God by praying these heartfelt prayers:

Oh, my patient Father, the tyranny of the urgent
seems so ever-present in my mind. As I kneel in your
presence, I lay down my to-dos, should-dos, want-
to-dos, and even can't-dos. But most of all, I bring
you my fragmented mind with its swirl of questions
and data and brokenness and demands and lay all—
my mind, body, soul, emotions, and spirit—in rest
at your feet. I lay this troubled head of mine on your

knee and choose to look only in your face for this sweet time. Now, in this moment, there is only you. I love you, my Jesus.[1]

—SANDI

My Lord and my God, listening is hard for me. I do not exactly mean hard, for I understand that this is a matter of receiving rather than trying. What I mean is that I am so action oriented, so product driven, that doing is easier for me than being. I need your help if I am to be still and listen. I would like to try. I would like to learn how to sink down into the light of your presence until I can become comfortable in that posture. Help me to try now.[2]

—RICHARD FOSTER

THE TWENTY-MINUTE
WORSHIP EXPERIENCE

I believe you will grow to appreciate the Twenty-Minute Worship Experience. Every day this week, be still before God for twenty minutes (if this seems like an impossibility, begin with ten minutes). If possible, be on your knees. (Yes, you can use a pillow!)

Here are some suggestions for your worship time:

1. Be honest: Tell God, "My Lord, I need You to teach me how to worship You."
2. Pray "The Prayer of Quiet."
3. Pray Psalm 131, asking God to reveal to you how your soul can be stilled.
4. Put on a headset and worship with worship music. Sing or say the music to your God.
5. Refer to "365 Names, Titles, and Attributes of the Father, Son, and Holy Spirit" on page 134.
6. As you spend time on your knees before God each day, journal about what He reveals to you as you worship.

MY DAILY REFLECTIONS

Surely I have composed and quieted my soul;
Like a weaned child rests against his mother,
My soul is like a weaned child within me.

PSALM 131:2

When you pray, listen to the silence. Silence is a gift. There is power in silence. There is also a reverential fear of God in silence. Silence is a time to regroup, rethink, reevaluate, and reflect. Silence is the selah of God. Selah is God's musical interlude, pausing in the symphony of life to stop, look, listen, and take some time to think about what has been sung. In silence there is music, and God has a song.

—PAT CHEN

Busyness is the enemy of spirituality. It is essentially laziness. It is doing the easy thing instead of the hard thing. It is filling our time with our own actions instead of paying attention to God's actions. It is taking charge.

—EUGENE PETERSON

_____

_____

_____

_____

_____

_____

_____

_____

_____

_____

_____

_____

_____

_____

_____

_____

_____

Learning to be quiet before the Lord is one of the greatest challenges we face today in our quest to enter in and experience true intimacy with Him.

—JAMES GOLL

My soul, wait in silence for God only,
For my hope is from Him.

PSALM 62:5

Rest. Rest. Rest in God's love. The only work
you are required now to do is to give your most
intense attention to His still, small voice within.

—MADAME JEANNE GUYON

I avoid stillness because stillness takes me to deeper places . . . places where I have pushed aside truths I did not want to face or believe . . . places where I have pushed hard things. Passion and pain live in still places. It takes courage to go to the place of stillness . . . courage and trust. I am afraid to go there. I approach worship with the same enthusiasm as exercise: If I can stay busy, I can avoid it.

—AN HONEST WOMAN

_____

_____

_____

_____

_____

_____

_____

_____

_____

_____

_____

_____

_____

_____

_____

_____

Though I am always in haste, I am never in a hurry;
because I never undertake any more work than I can
go through with perfect calmness of spirit.

—JOHN WESLEY

WHAT DID I LEARN ABOUT GOD THIS WEEK?

_____
_____
_____
_____
_____
_____
_____
_____

WHAT DID I LEARN ABOUT MYSELF THIS WEEK?

_____
_____
_____
_____
_____
_____
_____
_____

WHAT DID I LEARN ABOUT
WORSHIP THIS WEEK?

_____

_____

_____

_____

_____

_____

_____

_____

MY PRAYER EXPRESSING HOW I
LONG TO LEARN STILLNESS BEFORE GOD:

_____

_____

_____

_____

_____

_____

_____

_____

_____

Week Four

DRAWN INTO
HIS PRESENCE

Week Four

DRAWN INTO
HIS PRESENCE

He has satisfied the thirsty soul,
And the hungry soul He has filled with what
is good.

PSALM 107:9

When we started your worship journey, I said that worship begins in holy expectancy and ends in holy obedience. I also told you that hidden in worship is the presence of God.

I asked my friend Lorraine to tell you how she discovered God's presence.

How did I come to this place of knowing His presence?

At first, there was much effort. Like a hidden treasure, I searched Him out, pursuing every clue that would lead me to Him. I moved rocks and dirt, dug deep in God's Word, and attended every Bible study or conference that would reveal Him. God often rewarded my searching with precious nuggets and gems, but I knew that I had not yet found the whole of the treasure.

About ten years into the hunt, something changed. Almost imperceptibly, I became aware that my labor was no longer needed—that the treasure was not a destination but God Himself. Daily, He brought the treasure of His presence to me. Labor ceased. We simply enjoyed each other. Sometimes we shared the depths of comfort and laughter that is shared between lifelong friends. Other times we shared the passions and dreams of two intimate lovers. Still other times, it was the excitement of discovery as an all-wise teacher revealed hidden secrets to an eager student.

He has become all things to me: Father, Friend. Lover, Teacher. Companion, Holy Ruler. I am as comfortable bowing down to Him in fear and trembling as I am snuggling in His arms.

He is the breath in my lungs, the blood in my veins, the passion of my heart, and the fulfillment of all my longings.[1]

THE TWENTY-MINUTE
WORSHIP EXPERIENCE

This week I would like you to look back. Spend time looking through the *Satisfy My Thirsty Soul Journal.*

Each day during your Twenty-Minute Worship Experience, thank God for all He has taught you about Himself, all you have learned about YOU, and all you have learned about worship.

Here are other suggestions for your worship time:

1. Be honest: Tell God, "My Lord, I want to go deeper in knowing your presence."
2. Worship God with Psalms 16, 42, and 89.
3. Put on a headset and worship with worship music. Sing or say the music to your God.

MY DAILY REFLECTIONS

*The beauty of bowing everything as an act of worship
is that we discover His presence in the most mundane
of places (like writing an email or pruning roses).
I love this! My life can become my love song to Jesus!*

—A WORSHIPER

_____

_____

_____

_____

_____

_____

_____

_____

_____

_____

_____

_____

_____

_____

*By dwelling in the presence of God, I have established
such a sweet communion with the Lord that my spirit
abides, without much effort, in the restful peace
of God. In this rest, I am filled with faith that equips
me to handle anything that comes to me.*

—BROTHER LAWRENCE

*Happy are those who hear the joyful call to worship,
for they will walk in the light of your presence, LORD.*

PSALM 89:15, NLT

Over the last ten years, I have chased after His presence with all my strength. As I have chosen to run to Him rather than running away from Him, I have experienced a far deeper intimacy with Him than I had ever imagined. How have I done this? Through practicing His presence and making worship a priority.

—BECKY HARLING

The four living creatures, each one of them having six wings, are full of eyes around and within; and day and night they do not cease to say,

"HOLY, HOLY, HOLY IS THE LORD GOD, THE ALMIGHTY, WHO WAS AND WHO IS AND WHO IS TO COME."

REVELATION 4:8

The Spirit and the bride say, "Come." And let the one who hears say, "Come." And let the one who is thirsty come; let the one who wishes take the water of life without cost.

REVELATION 22:17

_____
_____
_____
_____
_____
_____
_____
_____
_____
_____
_____
_____
_____
_____
_____
_____
_____
_____

Often someone who knows the Lord intimately will make us painfully hungry for a higher and deeper experience of Christ. It is the greatest of all influences, to provoke another believer to thirst as a deer after the waterbrook.

God is more real to me than any thought or thing or person. . . . I feel Him in the sunshine or rain. . . . I talk to Him as to a companion. I pray and praise, and our communion is delightful. He answers me again and again, often in words so clearly spoken that it seems my outer ear must have carried the tone, but generally in strong mental impressions. He speaks to me through the Scripture and unfolds some new view of Him and His love for me. The truth that He is mine and I am His never leaves me; it is an abiding joy.

—WILLIAM JAMES

I have only begun to grow as a worshiper. I thought I knew about worship, but this pursuit will take my whole life. Worship is what I was made for, what each of us were made for.

—A WISE WOMAN

_____

_____

_____

_____

_____

_____

_____

_____

_____

_____

_____

_____

_____

_____

_____

_____

_____

_____

_____

Then I looked, and I heard the voice of many angels around the throne and the living creatures and the elders; and the number of them was myriads of myriads, and thousands of thousands, saying with a loud voice,

"Worthy is the Lamb that was slain to receive power and riches and wisdom and might and honor and glory and blessing."

REVELATION 5:11-12

WHAT DID I LEARN ABOUT
GOD THIS WEEK?

_____

_____

_____

_____

_____

_____

_____

_____

WHAT DID I LEARN ABOUT
MYSELF THIS WEEK?

_____

_____

_____

_____

_____

_____

_____

_____

WHAT DID I LEARN ABOUT
WORSHIP THIS WEEK?

_____

_____

_____

_____

_____

_____

_____

_____

MY PRAYER ABOUT HOW I LONG TO
CONTINUE GROWING AS A WORSHIPER
AND WALKING IN GOD'S PRESENCE:

_____

_____

_____

_____

_____

_____

_____

_____

_____

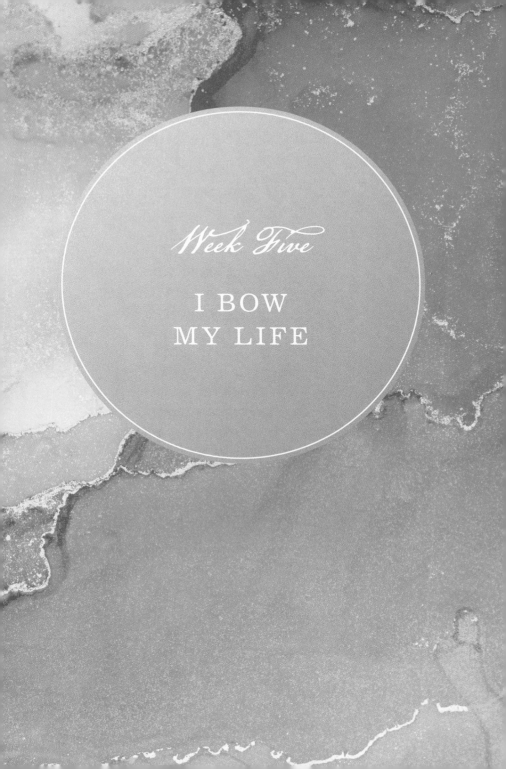

Week Five

I BOW
MY LIFE

I BOW MY LIFE

βome, let us worship and bow down,
Let us bow our lives before God.

PSALM 95:6, AUTHOR'S PARAPHRASE

Worship is the specific act of bowing my knees and declaring, "Holy, Holy, Holy." Worship is also a *lifestyle* of bowing my life and living "holy, holy, holy." Every day you and I have an opportunity and privilege to bow every area of our lives before our King. As I have lived out my worship, it has elevated my choices of obedience before my God. Truly, worship is the lifestyle of a grateful heart.

To worship is to respond; worship is the response of our heart to our Lover. What is my love response to the One who has given all? I can only bow before Him every day. I bow my life, my words, my attitude, my work, my pain, and my will. But the foundation is that I first bow my life.

My friend Sandi expressed the surrender of Romans 12:1 like this:

> I respond to your urgency, Lord, by laying down this
> body, soul, and spirit of mine, which in actuality is

yours, but I acknowledge your ownership and release my claim, trusting in your mercy and all you are. I offer this to you as what I can bring to your altar in worship . . . joyfully, expectantly, out of longing to make your heart glad.[1]

My friend Kathy expressed her surrender in this way:

When I at last gave my final percentages to God, I did the releasing from what felt like my grave. But losing the extra weight of that burden helped me crawl out of my pit and learn how to fully live! A life surrendered through crucifixion unto Jesus is a life fully resurrected by grace. Giving those final pieces of my old life hurt tremendously, but He wants all of me. The glory of God is a person fully alive, and I feel more alive than ever![2]

THE TWENTY-MINUTE
WORSHIP EXPERIENCE

I hope falling to your knees and worshiping is becoming more comfortable for you. Again, I encourage you to practice the Twenty-Minute Worship Experience this week. Be still before God for twenty minutes every day. If possible, be on your knees.

Here are some suggestions for your worship time:

1. Be honest: Tell God, "My Lord, I need You to teach me how to worship You by bowing my life to You."
2. Pray Psalm 139, asking God to reveal insights to how He created you!
3. Take a "holy hike" and spontaneously worship God as you walk.
4. Put on a headset and worship with worship music. Sing or say the music to your God.
5. As you spend time on your knees before God each day, write down in this journal what God reveals about who He is and what surrender looks like for you.

MY DAILY REFLECTIONS

A summary of Psalm 25:14 and John 14:21:

To fear my Lord is to obey Him;
To obey my Lord is to worship Him;
To worship my Lord is to surrender my All;
To surrender my All is to love Him;
To love my Lord is to be His friend;
To be a friend of my Lord is to be His confidante;
To be a confidante of my Lord is to share His secrets;
To share the secrets of my Lord is to be intimate with Him.
O how Amazing, how Incredible, how Inconceivable
To have the privilege
   The opportunity
      The invitation
         The ecstasy
            Of such a relationship
With the Almighty God of the Ages.
How can it be that the unworthy be made so worthy
   By One so Holy?[3]

—CHEE-HWA

_____

_____

_____

_____

_____

_____

_____

*Obedience out of love is a doorway to more of Him.
Worship draws us into an ever-deepening knowledge of
His Being. Obedience draws us into an ever-deepening
understanding of His ways. Both are acts of love.
Together they draw us into an ever-deepening love
relationship with our Beloved.*

—A WISE WOMAN

My heart I give Thee, eagerly and sincerely.

—SEAL OF JOHN CALVIN

Worship is the submission of all our nature to God.
It is the quickening of conscience by His holiness,
The nourishment of mind with His truth,
The purifying of imagination by His beauty,
The opening of the heart to His love,
The surrender of will to His purpose,
And all this gathered up in adoration.

—WILLIAM TEMPLE

What can I give Him,
Poor as I am?
If I were a shepherd
I would bring a lamb.
If I were a Wise Man
I would do my part—
Yet what I can I give Him,
Give my heart.

— CHRISTINA GEORGINA ROSSETTI

Worship is to be lived in the context of a twenty-four seven relationship to the Giver of all things.

—A WORSHIPER

_____

_____

_____

_____

_____

_____

_____

_____

_____

_____

_____

_____

_____

_____

_____

_____

_____

_____

Look at all God has done for us! In light of the fact God gives us all and He is our all . . . is it too much for Him to ask us to offer our bodies as a sacrifice of worship?

—A WISE WOMAN

If you obey my commands, you will remain in my love, just as I have obeyed my Father's commands and remain in his love.

JOHN 15:10, NIV

The secret [of the sweet, satisfying companionship] of the Lord have they who fear (revere and worship) Him, and He will show them His covenant and reveal to them its [deep, inner] meaning.

PSALM 25:14, AMPC

*I bow my life in worship, and my life declares,
"Holy, Holy, Holy!"*

---

*I don't have daily devotionals anymore; I have
"daily desperations"! I need the Word of God on
an almost intravenous feeding plan.*

—AN HONEST WOMAN

Where do I worship? Sometimes my mind is my place of worship, and in the middle of everything, I just let my being worship.

—SANDI

_____

_____

_____

_____

_____

_____

_____

_____

_____

_____

_____

_____

_____

_____

_____

_____

_____

WHAT DID I LEARN ABOUT
GOD THIS WEEK?

_____
_____
_____
_____
_____
_____
_____
_____
_____

WHAT DID I LEARN ABOUT
MYSELF THIS WEEK?

_____
_____
_____
_____
_____
_____
_____
_____
_____

WHAT DID I LEARN ABOUT
WORSHIP THIS WEEK?

_____

_____

_____

_____

_____

_____

_____

_____

MY PRAYER ABOUT BOWING
MY LIFE IN WORSHIP:

_____

_____

_____

_____

_____

_____

_____

_____

_____

_____

_____

Week Six

I BOW
MY WORDS

Week Six

I BOW MY WORDS

Come, let us worship and bow down,
Let us bow our words before God.

PSALM 95:6, AUTHOR'S PARAPHRASE

Our words have power—power for good or evil. A kind word picks up a person who is weighed down by trouble. One wise woman paraphrased Proverbs 18:21, which talks about our words, in this thought-provoking way:

> Our words are like vitamins or poison. When we speak kind, true, encouraging words, it's as if we give the people we are talking to very strong vitamins that make them have life and joy and energy. But, if we speak negative, harsh, unkind, untrue words, it's as if we are feeding them poison, and it results in their cells dying.

We have such a privilege—we can pour encouragement into those God has given us to love. And when we bless those made in God's image, we are also blessing Him. What joy!

My desire is that I never break God's heart with my words. I believe that this is your desire as well. May we grow to bless and encourage all those God brings along our path.

THE TWENTY-MINUTE
WORSHIP EXPERIENCE

I hope falling to your knees and worshiping is becoming more and more heartening to you. Again, I encourage you to practice the Twenty-Minute Worship Experience this week. Be still before Him for twenty minutes every day.

Here are some suggestions for your worship time:

1. Be honest: Tell God, "My Lord, I need You to teach me how to worship You with my words."
2. Pray Psalms 66 and 71.
3. Put on a headset and worship with worship music. Sing or say the music to your God.
4. Worship God with "365 Names, Titles, and Attributes of the Father, Son, and Holy Spirit" (see page 134).
5. As you spend time on your knees before God each day, write down what God reveals to you about who He is and about what bowing your words in worship looks like for you.

MY DAILY REFLECTIONS

A gentle answer turns away wrath,
But a harsh word stirs up anger.
The tongue of the wise makes knowledge acceptable,
But the mouth of fools spouts folly. . . .
A soothing tongue is a tree of life,
But perversion in it crushes the spirit.

PROVERBS 15:1-2, 4

_____

_____

_____

_____

_____

_____

_____

_____

_____

_____

_____

_____

_____

_____

*Death and life are in the power of the tongue,
And those who love it will eat its fruit.*

PROVERBS 18:21

He who restrains his words has knowledge.

PROVERBS 17:27

The heart of the wise instructs his mouth
And adds persuasiveness to his lips.
Pleasant words are a honeycomb,
Sweet to the soul and healing to the bones.

PROVERBS 16:23-24

It is much wiser to choose what you say than to say what you choose.
The written word can be erased —not so with the spoken word.

One of my definitions of worship is offering back to God as a sacrifice all the goodness and blessings He has given me. If I am pulling garbage out of my heart and spewing it forth, I certainly don't believe God would consider it worship.

—KATHY

*God not only desires me to worship Him with beautiful
words of praise—that's easy—but He also desires
me to worship Him with my words to others as well.
That one is HARD!*

—BEV

_____

_____

_____

_____

_____

_____

_____

_____

_____

_____

_____

_____

_____

_____

_____

_____

_____

Like apples of gold in settings of silver
Is a word spoken in right circumstances.

PROVERBS 25:11

It's better to live alone in the corner of an attic
than with a quarrelsome wife in a lovely home.

PROVERBS 21:9, NLT

WHAT DID I LEARN ABOUT
GOD THIS WEEK?

_____

_____

_____

_____

_____

_____

_____

_____

WHAT DID I LEARN ABOUT
MYSELF THIS WEEK?

_____

_____

_____

_____

_____

_____

_____

_____

WHAT DID I LEARN ABOUT
WORSHIP THIS WEEK?

_____

_____

_____

_____

_____

_____

_____

MY PRAYER ABOUT HOW I LONG TO
BOW MY WORDS IN WORSHIP:

_____

_____

_____

_____

_____

_____

_____

_____

Week Seven

I BOW
MY ATTITUDE

Week Seven

I BOW MY ATTITUDE

Come, let us worship and bow down,
Let us bow our attitude before God.
PSALM 95:6, AUTHOR'S PARAPHRASE

God's Word shouts from cover to cover, "Be a thankful people; let it become such a part of your being that you *overflow with thankfulness*" (Colossians 2:7, author's paraphrase). Gratitude to God should be as regular as our heartbeats.

Kathy expressed her desire to not have an attitude of grumbling but an attitude of gratitude in the following prayer:

Lord, I want to live my life as a living sacrifice to you. When my attitude speaks more of my human nature than of my divine spirit, my sacrifice is tainted, and once again this living sacrifice crawls off the altar. Continue to work on my attitude, Lord. May I be positive and encouraging in all situations, not just those seen in the open but especially in situations behind closed doors where no one else will see. Help me to continue to be a woman of integrity so that my personality and attitude reflect who you are at all times.

My attitude is such a powerful witness of who you are in me. I pray I can worship you with an attitude of gratitude in all things.[1]

Giving thanks in all things has to become a daily habit. It is not natural for our hearts to overflow with thanksgiving. Every day we must make a secret choice to give thanks. One woman expressed it like this:

I am just like the Israelites. I so easily go from rejoicing to despair. Gratitude is exactly like the manna God gave the Jews. It does not carry from one day to the next but must be "gathered" or chosen fresh each morning.

May we become daily gatherers of the attitude of gratitude!

THE TWENTY-MINUTE
WORSHIP EXPERIENCE

I hope falling to your knees and worshiping is becoming more and more natural for you. Again, I encourage you to practice the Twenty-Minute Worship Experience this week. Be still before Him for twenty minutes every day.

Here are some suggestions for your worship time:

1. Be honest: Tell God, "My Lord, I need You to teach me how to worship You with my attitude."
2. Read Revelation 21 out loud and prayerfully.
3. Read Psalm 50 and meditate on it as you worship.
4. Put on a headset and worship with worship music. Sing or say the music to your God.
5. As you spend time on your knees before God each day, write down what God reveals to you about who He is and about what bowing your attitude in worship looks like for you.

MY DAILY REFLECTIONS

The man who forgets to
be thankful has fallen asleep in life.

—ROBERT LOUIS STEVENSON

_____

_____

_____

_____

_____

_____

_____

_____

_____

_____

_____

_____

_____

_____

_____

_____

_____

_____

Thanksgiving is our dialect.

EPHESIANS 5:4, MSG

No duty is more urgent than that of returning thanks.

—SAINT AMBROSE

*The most important prayer in the world
is just two words long: "Thank you."*

—MEISTER ECKHART

_____

_____

_____

_____

_____

_____

_____

_____

_____

_____

_____

_____

*The worship most acceptable to God comes
from a thankful and cheerful heart.*

—PLUTARCH

*Gratitude takes nothing for granted, is never unresponsive,
is constantly awakening to new wonder, and
to praise of the goodness of God.*

—THOMAS MERTON

*A smart woman said,
"Being thankful gives me energy."*

*Reading the Psalms always moves me toward
gratitude. Sometimes I have to read a psalm
three or four times before I begin to agree
with David in his gratitude.*

—AN HONEST WOMAN

*Attitude is the speaker of our present;
it is the prophet of our future.*

—JOHN C. MAXWELL

My Lord, how I long to live in constant acknowledgment of who you are by being always grateful. But . . . sadly, I am weak and myopic. I yearn for this life of mine to be a dance of gratitude to you, my Beloved.

—ONE WOMAN'S PRAYER

_____

_____

_____

_____

_____

_____

_____

_____

_____

_____

_____

_____

Giving a "sacrifice of praise" means emptying myself of my agenda and what I think is right for my day and instead seeing any detour in my plan as the gift of His plan.

—A WISE WOMAN

The soul that gives thanks can find
comfort in everything; the soul that
complains can find comfort in nothing.

—HANNAH WHITALL SMITH

It's not so much what happens to us,
as what happens in us that counts.

—TIM HANSEL

Lord, can I be bold enough to thank you for hardship? Hearts molded in your refining fire will never be the same. I praise you for smoothing and softening my heart more and more every day into the image of the heart of Jesus. Lord, I praise you for holding hearts when they could have been shattered. My praise comes from a heart full of joy. All praise and glory and honor be to the One who knows everything about me . . . and loves me anyway.

—ONE WOMAN'S THANKFUL PSALM

WHAT DID I LEARN ABOUT
GOD THIS WEEK?

_____

_____

_____

_____

_____

_____

_____

_____

WHAT DID I LEARN ABOUT
MYSELF THIS WEEK?

_____

_____

_____

_____

_____

_____

_____

_____

WHAT DID I LEARN ABOUT
WORSHIP THIS WEEK?

_____

_____

_____

_____

_____

_____

_____

_____

MY PRAYER EXPRESSING HOW I DESIRE TO
BOW MY ATTITUDE IN WORSHIP:

_____

_____

_____

_____

_____

_____

_____

_____

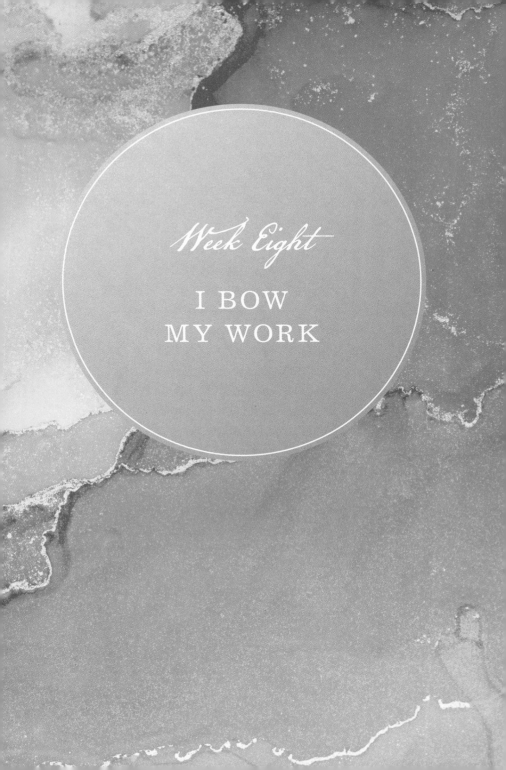

Week Eight

I BOW
MY WORK

Week Eight

I BOW MY WORK

Come, let us worship and bow down,
Let us bow our work before God.

PSALM 95:6, AUTHOR'S PARAPHRASE

It has been said that approximately half our waking hours are spent working. (Many women would laugh at this estimate— seven-eighths would be more like it!) In light of this, we would benefit from developing a new and higher view of work.

This Latin phrase gives us a new perspective of work: *Laborare est orare. Orare est laborare.* Translated it means, "To work is to worship. To worship is to work." How wonderful to see our creative *and* mundane work as an opportunity to bow in worship. Each of our moments of work, bowed before God, not only gives joy to others but is counted as worship to the Holy One.

When asked how she described work and worship, one wise woman said:

What is worship? It is taking the part of my life called work and placing it on the altar as my offering to my God because I love Him. This is my spiritual act of worship.

May we live Colossians 3:23-24:

Whatever you do, do your work heartily, as for the Lord rather than for men, knowing that from the Lord you will receive the reward of the inheritance. It is the Lord Christ whom you serve.

THE TWENTY-MINUTE WORSHIP EXPERIENCE

I hope you are beginning to want to fall to your knees and worship. Again, I encourage you to practice the Twenty-Minute Worship Experience this week. Be still before Him for twenty minutes every day.

Here are some suggestions for your worship time:

1. Be honest: Tell God, "My Lord, I need You to teach me how to worship You with my work."
2. Meditate in your worship time on Psalms 5, 16, and 90.
3. Worship with the ABCs of Worship.
4. Put on a headset and worship with worship music. Sing or say the music to your God.
5. As you spend time on your knees before God each day, write down what God reveals to you about who He is and about what it looks like for you to bow your work in worship.

MY DAILY REFLECTIONS

When physical, mundane work seems tedious, remember: God did physical labor. He created the world out of nothing, but He also planted a garden (Genesis 2:8-9), heaved the giant door of Noah's ark shut (Genesis 7:16), and even acts as a cook (Psalm 104:27-28)! The only thing we know about the Lord Jesus from ages twelve to thirty is that He worked with His hands as a carpenter. This was His "spiritual" preparation for ministry.

I have brought you glory on earth by completing the
work you gave me to do.

JOHN 17:4, NIV

_____

_____

_____

_____

_____

_____

_____

_____

_____

_____

_____

_____

_____

_____

Before this study I believed that sitting at the
feet of Jesus was spiritual and that preparing
meals was not. Now I see that EVERYTHING
I do can be an offering to the Lord.

—BEV

Work is worship;
God . . .
Takes our toils for homage sweet
And accepts as signs of worship
Well-worn hands and wearied feet.

—THE MONK ELMO

Oswald Chambers had this beautiful thought about our work: We are to worship, wait, and then work.

_____

_____

_____

_____

_____

_____

_____

_____

_____

_____

_____

_____

_____

_____

_____

_____

_____

_____

_____

_____

_____

_____

Brother Lawrence had it figured out. He knew who he was working for. "We ought not to be weary of doing little things for the love of God, who regards not the greatness of the work, but the love with which it is performed."

A Mother's Prayer

My Lord, so much of being a mother at home is servant's work. It requires no special skill, and it never ends. Working outside the home was so much easier. But Lord, I accept your assignment. I bow my cleaning to you as my daily act of worship. You—not my husband nor my children—are my employer. Your favor and presence is my reward. I invite you into my work of service toward my family, not just in the teachable moments of mothering but in the daily work of creating a haven for my loved ones. I worship you under the kitchen table as I clean up crumbs, I worship you as I potty train, help with homework, feed hungry children, and teach my son not to bite his sister. I worship you in this "work" because it has all been assigned by you.[1]

—CHEE-HWA

WHAT DID I LEARN ABOUT
GOD THIS WEEK?

_____
_____
_____
_____
_____
_____
_____
_____

WHAT DID I LEARN ABOUT
MYSELF THIS WEEK?

_____
_____
_____
_____
_____
_____
_____
_____

WHAT DID I LEARN ABOUT
WORSHIP THIS WEEK?

_____

_____

_____

_____

_____

_____

_____

_____

_____

MY PRAYER EXPRESSING HOW I LONG TO
BOW MY WORK IN WORSHIP:

_____

_____

_____

_____

_____

_____

_____

_____

_____

Week Nine

I BOW
MY PAIN

Week Nine

I BOW MY PAIN

ℂome, let us worship and bow down,
Let us bow our pain before God.

PSALM 95:6, AUTHOR'S PARAPHRASE

A man once drew some black dots. No one could make anything of them but an irregular assemblage of black dots. Then he drew a few lines, put in a few rests, then a clef at the beginning, and it became clear that the black dots were musical notes for the doxology:

Praise God from whom all blessings flow,
Praise Him all creatures here below.

Each of us has many black dots and black spots in our lives. We cannot understand *why* they are there or *why* God permitted them to come. But if we let Him adjust the dots in the proper way, draw the lines He wants, and put in the rests at the appropriate places, then out of the black dots and spots in our lives, He will make a glorious harmony.

When I bow my pain, it is an act of worship. "But as for me, I *will* hope continually, and *will* praise You yet more and more!" (Psalm 71:14, emphasis added). Praise in our prisons of pain is a high form of worship. As C. H. Spurgeon says, "Our griefs cannot mar the melody of our praise; they are simply the bass notes of our life song: To God Be the Glory."[1]

May we grow in bowing our pain in worship so our life song will become "To God Be the Glory!"

THE TWENTY-MINUTE
WORSHIP EXPERIENCE

Is worship beginning to be part of your life? I hope so! Again, I encourage you to practice the Twenty-Minute Worship Experience this week. Be still before Him for twenty minutes every day.

Here are some suggestions for your worship time:

1. Be honest: Tell God, "My Lord, this is hard! I need You to teach me how to worship You in my pain."
2. Meditate and personalize Psalm 20.
3. Read and pray Psalm 142 out loud to God.
4. Read Psalm 27 and pray it personally to God.
5. Put on a headset and worship with worship music. Sing or say the music to God.
6. As you spend time on your knees before God each day, write down what God reveals to you about who He is and about what it looks like for you to bow your pain in worship. Be honest, and tell Him how hard it is to bow your pain.

MY DAILY REFLECTIONS

The pain of rejection and abandonment cause me to feel unloved and lonely, but God is using it to make me desperate for Him. He is coming to me as I worship, and the walls of fear and distrust are coming down in His presence.

—AN HONEST WOMAN

Afflictions are but the shadow of God's wings.

—GEORGE MACDONALD

He said not: thou shalt not be troubled,
thou shalt not be tempted, thou shalt not be distressed.
But He said, thou shalt not be overcome.

—JULIAN OF NORWICH

Sorrow is a fruit; God does not allow it
to grow on a branch that is too weak to bear it.

—VICTOR HUGO

When you are in the dark, listen, and
God will give you a very precious message
for someone else once you are back in the light.

—OSWALD CHAMBERS

*When one loves what God is doing in one's life,
one cannot hate the instrument through which it comes.*

—MADAME JEANNE GUYON

_____

_____

_____

_____

_____

_____

_____

_____

_____

_____

_____

_____

_____

_____

_____

*When you find yourself in the midst of pain, begin to
worship God. As we worship the Lord, the atmosphere
is changed. When Paul and Silas were in jail, their
songs of worship became a weapon against the enemy,
and the doors of their prison were opened wide.*

For in the day of trouble He will conceal me in
His tabernacle;
in the secret place of His tent He will hide me.

PSALM 27:5

Thank the good God for having visited you
through suffering; if we knew the value of
suffering, we would ask for it.

—BROTHER ANDREW

Never judge God by suffering,
but judge suffering by the cross.

—FATHER ANDREW

Have courage for the great sorrows of life,
and patience for the small ones. And when you
have laboriously accomplished your daily task,
go to sleep in peace. God is awake.

—VICTOR HUGO

For You light my lamp;
The LORD my God illumines my darkness.
For by You I can run upon a troop;
and by my God I can leap over a wall.

PSALM 18:28-29

The LORD is a shelter for the oppressed,
a refuge in times of trouble.

PSALM 9:9, NLT

_A season of suffering is a small price
to pay for a clear view of God._

—MAX LUCADO

God is our refuge and strength, a very present help in trouble. Therefore we will not fear.

PSALM 46:1-2, ESV

WHAT DID I LEARN ABOUT
GOD THIS WEEK?

_____

_____

_____

_____

_____

_____

_____

_____

WHAT DID I LEARN ABOUT
MYSELF THIS WEEK?

_____

_____

_____

_____

_____

_____

_____

_____

WHAT DID I LEARN ABOUT
WORSHIP THIS WEEK?

_____
_____
_____
_____
_____
_____
_____
_____

MY HONEST PRAYER ABOUT
THE "PAIN" OF BOWING MY PAIN TO GOD:

_____
_____
_____
_____
_____
_____
_____
_____
_____